Impact Greek

The Joy and Power of the Greek New Test

By

Pastor Kenneth R. Jones
Master of Arts in New Testament
Denver Seminary

ISBN: 978-1-4357-2370-2

July 1, 2008

"Scripture taken from the HOLY BIBLE, NEW INTERNATIONAL VERSION.
Copyright 1973, 1978, 1984 International Bible Society.
Used by permission of Zondervan Bible Publishers."

Copyright 2008 by Kenneth R. Jones

ISBN: 978-1-4357-2370-2

Ascription

To the Lord Jesus,
the returning King of Glory
(Psalm 24:7-10).

Dedication

To Pam,
my sweet, beautiful wife
who is also
the loving and exceptional mother of our three children . . .
Caleb Lukas, Micah Zachary and Hannah Grace.

Acknowledgements

I extend my thanks and appreciation to Caleb Jones, Micah Jones, Hannah Jones, Richard Webster, John Henning, David Dennis, Alice Dewhurst, John Sill, Joel Kuehn and Travis Little for contributing their enthusiastic support and expertise to this project.

Pastor Ken Jones in his study at the church (2007).

As the author of the *Impact Greek System of Study* in order to better learn New Testament Greek, Ken has prepared the following books to help people experience the joy of Greek:

- **Impact Greek: the Joy and Power of the Greek New Testament (Volume 1).**

- Gospel Road Pictures: An *Impact Greek* introduction to the Prepositions (Volume 2).

- Impact Greek for Today: Further Studies in the Greek of the New Testament (volume 3).

- The Awe, Art and Attitude of the Lord's Prayer in the Greek New Testament (Volume 4).

E-mail **impactgreek@hotmail.com** if you would like further information about these resources.

Outline

Introduction to New Testament Greek

Chapter One: Impact Greek for the Pastor and the People of God

Chapter Two: Why did God choose Greek to communicate the Gospel of His Son?

Investigation of New Testament Greek

Chapter Three: How to be an Expert in saying "No" in Greek

Chapter Four: The H.O.P.E. Bible Study Method with the O.P.E.N. Journal

Insights into New Testament Greek

Chapter Five: Calligraphy Greek

Chapter Six: The Autographs of God

Chapter Seven: Theological Greek

Introduction to New Testament Greek

Greek for the Pastor and the People of God

Learning Greek, the original language of the New Testament, is vital for the ministry.[1] Every minister must be committed to becoming skillful in the field of exegesis of the Greek New Testament. Our congregations, which we guard and guide, depend on us for this so that they might experience some of the majestic gems of grace contained in the Greek New Testament. Greek grammar is a means of grace for the minister and his congregation. The great preachers of ancient and modern times would agree with this evaluation of the importance of the Greek.[2] In seminary, I was taught that the best way to show love for the people of God is to study hard for them so that my preaching, teaching and counsel might edify their heart. In this respect, it was essential to understand that the pastor doesn't have an office but a study. It's the pastor's study not the pastor's office that should be the nomenclature of a healthy, vital and faithful church. And in this time of study, I was encouraged to accompany that studious diligence with a heart devoted to praying for people. I found this to be exceptional, wise advice for the new pastor. Since then, I've seen this wisdom confirmed in my ministry multiple times. Also, the best way for a congregation to show love to their pastor is to support his study of the Word by prayer, financial provisions and protection of his study time. The pastor who loves God and His people and the church who loves God and their pastor will make the faithful exegesis of the Bible the key priority on all their calendars. If this is done, God will richly bless both pastor and congregation. So, I believe that there are at least five good reasons for local churches to pursue a diligent, devoted study in the Greek grammar of the New Testament as the following review indicates:

1. Power: Studying the Greek of the New Testament is Spiritually Empowering

- Apologetics

Martin Luther stated that:

> the simple preacher (it is true) has so many clear passages and texts available through translations that he can know and teach Christ, lead a holy life, and preach to others. But when it comes to interpreting Scripture, and working with it on your own, and ***disputing with those who cite it incorrectly***, he is unequal to the task; that cannot be done without languages as a sacred ark.[3] (Emphasis added)

John Piper agrees and writes, "We have, by and large, lost the biblical vision of a pastor as one who is mighty in the Scriptures, apt to teach, ***competent to confute opponents*** and able to penetrate to the unity of the whole counsel of God."[4] (Emphasis added) Pastor Piper says we have allowed others to fight the battles for us. It's no longer the local parish pastor fighting heretics of the day from his own Greek New Testament but its professors in seminaries. The problem with this, of course, is that each church doesn't have a live professor of Greek sitting in the pews to give you, the local parish pastor, back-up when the heretic decides to cause havoc in your church. The bottom line here is this: if you love your people and desire to protect the glory of God then you'll learn your language skills to drive the wolves far away and deepen the faith of the sheep.

- Spiritual Warfare

Martin Luther made this startling statement:

> The devil does not respect my spirit as highly as he does my speech and pen when they deal with Scripture. For my spirit takes from him nothing but myself alone; but Holy Scripture *and the languages* leave him little room on earth, and wreak havoc in his kingdom. (Emphasis added)

Luther believed that the Devil was most scared of him when he would exegete the Scripture from its original language (Hebrew or Greek). Do you want the full impact of the armor of God? Then use the Sword of the Spirit—the Word of God—in its original language. As Martin Luther said, "The Languages are the sheath in which the sword of the Spirit is contained." Therefore, proper expository exposition from the Greek or the Hebrew is a service of praise to God, a shield of faith for your congregation, and a scourge to Satan and his devious plans.

- Inspired Preaching/Teaching

John Piper observes:

> Another result when pastors do not study the Bible in Greek and Hebrew is that they (and their churches with them) tend to become second-handers. . . We may impress one another for a while by dropping the name of the latest book, but second-hand food will not sustain and deepen our people's faith and holiness.

Or as Martin Luther exhorts:

> Therefore, although faith and the gospel may indeed be proclaimed by simple preachers without knowledge of the languages, such preaching is flat and tame; people finally become weary and bored with it, and it falls to the ground. **But where the preacher is versed in the languages, there is a freshness and vigor in his preaching,** Scripture is treated in its entirety, and faith finds itself constantly renewed by a continual variety of words and illustrations. (Emphasis added)

Again, we show the most love to our congregations when we labor in the original languages to bring the good news home to them from the far away land of heaven. The greatest compliment I've ever been given was from my youngest son, Micah, who is known as a man of few words. Even so, he once wrote me," Dad, you are the best preacher in the world. I like it when you preach the Word of God." Notice the second sentence. He likes my preaching because it is an exposition of the Word of God. Every pastor in God's kingdom can be the greatest preacher in the world if, and only if, they stay true to the Holy Biblical text.

2. Joy: Reading the Greek New Testament is a High and Holy Blessing

Dr. Walter Kaiser writes:

> The reading of the Bible in the original tongues of Greek and Hebrew was seen as a prerequisite for the Protestant ministry in the life of this nation during its earliest days. Evangelicalism can be no less dedicated to the same principle of studying the original languages. The reason for this undertaking has little, if anything, to do with tradition or an outmoded scholasticism. It is, rather, that no translation is inerrant; the appeal to inerrancy can only be to the original texts as represented by the best Greek and Hebrew manuscripts. As the Jewish poet Haim Nacham Bialik put it, ***"Reading the bible in translation is like kissing your bride through a veil."***[5] (Emphasis added)

It's that simple, fellow preachers! True joy and true love are relational, intimate, and conversational. Those in love are listening for their lover's unique, exquisite voice. If your heart's desire is to know God the best way you can, then there is no excuse for not digging into the original language of His Word.

As A.T. Robertson urges:

> We must never forget that in dealing with the words of Jesus we are dealing with things that have life and breath. That is true of all the New Testament, the most wonderful of all books of all time. One can feel the very throb of the heart of Almighty God in the New Testament if the eyes of his own heart have been enlightened by the Holy Spirit.[6]

Eugene Peterson, author of *The Message* Bible paraphrase, encourages Christians to read the Bible the way a dog chews on and plays with a bone, groaning with pleasure.[7]

3. Leadership: Skills of Guidance, Wisdom and Discernment

Dr. Piper asks, "Yet what is more important and more deeply *practical* for the pastoral office than advancing in Greek and Hebrew exegesis by which we mine God's treasures?" Indeed there isn't anything more important. In the case of Greek it has been known to sharpen the leadership skills of men to make them into great statesmen. Here's how Dr. Robertson explains it:

> In Dean West's volume, *The Value of the Classics*, the most striking argument is the one by business men, captains of industry, who plead for the retention of Latin and Greek in the college curriculum on the ground that classical students make better leaders in business life than those without the humanities. And ex-President Woodrow Wilson is quoted in a recent magazine as saying that, if he had his college course to do over, he would give more attention to the study of Greek.[8]

As Ulrich Zwingli, of the Reformation said:

> But a man cannot rightly order his own soul unless he exercises himself day and night in the Word of God. He can do that most readily if he is well versed in such languages as Hebrew and Greek . . . for languages are gifts of the Holy Spirit . . . If a man would penetrate to the heavenly wisdom . . . it is with such arms that he must be equipped. And even then he must still approach with a humble and thirsting spirit.[9]

In a word, learning Greek provides creditability for the minister's teaching ministry as H. H. Rowley observed;

> One who made it his life's work to interpret French literature, but who could only read it in English translation, would not be taken seriously; yet it is remarkable how many ministers of religion week by week expound a literature that they are unable to read save in translation.[10]

There is a moral gravitas in the above quotes. President Wilson recommends the knowledge of Greek in order to obtain superior discernment as a leader. Zwingli refers the pastor to the Greek New Testament in order to maintain a well-governed soul. Rowley remarks that a lack of knowledge of the original languages of Scripture could damage the minister's reputation as a competent scholar. Here then are three weighty arguments for the practical value of knowing the Greek language of the New Testament.

4. Growth: Holy Spirit Unction and Church Health

Mr. Kenneth S. Wuest states the positive news that the doctrine of the illumination of the Holy Spirit in the Greek New Testament is available for every minister:

> The Holy Spirit can give one a pair of Greek eyes to see, a Greek mind to think and a Greek tongue to expound the wonders of truth in the Greek text. The riches of the Greek New Testament are not reserved only for the pastor who has a brilliant mind and scholarly gifts. The Holy Spirit, the Great Interpreter, is able to make these available to the average Greek student of the Word.[11]

In fact, Wuest concludes his book, *The Practical Use of the Greek New Testament*, with these encouraging words:

> When the Holy Spirit finds an expositor who has been trained in Greek, and who is willing to do the exhaustive, hard, laborious and pain-staking study in the Greek New Testament, when He finds that that expositor is living a life of personal holiness and separation, a life fully yielded, and that the expositor desires a deep and thorough knowledge of the Greek New Testament in order that the Lord Jesus might be glorified in his exposition of the Word, then things happen.[12]

The result of such a diligent attention to the details of the Greek Text produces a Spirit-filled pastor who is filled with the very words given by the Holy Spirit as they are found in the Greek New Testament. In turn, the health of the congregation is improved because of their faithful involvement in hearing the exposition of the Greek New Testament as it was originally inspired by the Spirit of God.[13]

5. Recreation: A time of relaxation, refreshment and enjoyment.

It's been about 20 years since I've graduated from seminary. I've served five churches since that time. The best antidote to burnout or having a breakdown for me has always been my consistent retreat to the Greek New Testament. It's true that for each of my sermons I consult the original language of the Greek or the Hebrew to penetrate its riches with the help of the Holy Spirit. That's important and an essential aspect of a preacher's calling. However, that's not what I'm talking about here. I'm referring to simply having a personal time of Bible reading for my own edification and enjoyment. It is a time of recreation that I look forward too as though I was a kid again playing baseball with my buddies. It's God, me and the Greek text of the New Testament. As I read with my eyes and hear with my ears God's Word in its original format, it's hard for my bitterness, disappointments, and struggles not to evaporate in the spiritual heat of its heavenly rays.

I contend it's impossible to read the New Testament Greek account of Jesus' second coming (Revelation 19), the astonishing love of God (Romans 5) or the security of believers (Romans 8) without edifying changes occurring in your soul. Moreover, I assert that it's impossible to read those great Scriptures in the Greek without getting an inner rush that is more exciting than any sporting contest known to man. I've discovered especially that the Greek of the New Testament is truly a means of grace to my soul.[14] Even so, the most rewarding times of Bible reading have been when I've discovered something in the Greek text that applies to me in a personal, specific and sometimes humorous way. I'm constantly amazed how the Almighty God meets me in this sacred language. The Holy Spirit has moved me, molded me but mostly healed me of so many imperfections within my soul. You wouldn't know it by meeting me—you'd think that the Greek New Testament hasn't done its work of sanctification on me. This simply shows how far I need to travel. Nonetheless, I can truly testify that the nuances, precision and power of the Greek have made a huge impact in my inner world.

In the Greek New Testament I've heard the tones of God's love, the sounds of Christ's victory, and seen the sights of the Spirit's creativity. To read the Greek New Testament is truly to have a reverent conversation with the Holy Trinity.[15] The Greek New Testament is a means of grace. It shines for the searcher a light from a far distant yet altogether better place. It conveys blessings to those seeking its treasures. It will make you work for these pearls of wisdom. But it's an equal opportunity employer who hires all that sincerely come to it and rewards them for their honest toil with its cherished riches. My prayer is that, in the not too distant future, God will convince large numbers of the modern Christian world of the grandeur of the Greek New Testament and the joy of reading it. Now my six year old daughter, Hannah, when she sees me reading my maroon UBS Greek New Testament, often asks me, "Are you reading your Greek Bible, Dad?" Someday I'll be asking my daughter, "Are you reading your Greek Bible, Hannah?" And she'll know the joy of at least opening up her Greek interlinear and gazing upon the perfections contained therein.

How much light have our people lost (or our families) who have not been introduced to the Greek of the New Testament? This squandering of such Grace-bestowed treasure is simply not spiritually healthy for the people of God. A new reformation among God's people must reverse this course. I long for the day when the people in the pews will demand with energy and excitement that they be given insights into the Greek of the New Testament. As Pastor-scholar John Stott preaches on 1 Thessalonians 5:10, "The Holy Spirit is light as well as fire and, far from extinguishing him, we must let him both shine and burn within us."[16] Until the people of the Book become fired up with the Holy-Spirit-Inspired-Word in its original language; it's up to the preacher of God's Word to diligently, enthusiastically and competently convey the great nuggets of truth found in the amazing written record of God's Gospel of His beloved Son—the Greek New Testament.

It is my prayer and hope that this *Impact Greek* introduction will serve as a catalyst to further the interest of the people of God towards the edifying Greek of the New Testament. This book is designed to be like a wine tasting event where you are able to sip on the fine wines of a particular vineyard. But in this case, it's the spiritual wines of the vineyard of the Greek New Testament that you will be sampling. Come taste and see that the New Testament Greek of A.D. 30-95 was the best vintage ever produced— yet remarkably still available to all.

Decide now to commit the time necessary to delve into this *Impact Greek* book in order to experience a devotional blessing as you encounter God in the Greek pages of the infallible New Testament. If you give learning Greek a try in the manner that is presented in the following pages you'll discover that it will improve your individual times of Bible study. But more importantly it will improve your spiritual ability to teach God's truth. At one point in America's history our high school students were taught Greek. It was simply considered vital to a proper education. In fact the Greek Institute in Greece writes, "The Greek language is Greece's most precious gift to the world. The loftiest ideas and most refined sentiments have been expressed through the Greek language." That is why Greek was so essential to an excellent education. Today we have lost the academic and spiritual commitment to the essential importance of the Greek language providentially provided by God to proclaim the Gospel to the whole world of different languages.[17] Perhaps, by the illumination of the Holy Spirit, the Christian church in America and around the world will bring back this conviction that to be thoroughly educated in God's Holy Word you must have an introduction to the Greek language of the New Testament.

Here at the church I pastor I've seen a microcosm of this reformation in the Greek New Testament that so many long for. I offered this *Impact Greek* course to the church expecting about two members to participate. Fortunately, my faithless inclinations were wrong—54 adult Christians attended. Among them were 10 college students from Western Carolina University and 5 members from Cornerstone Evangelical Presbyterian, which is a sister church in town. The rest were members of my congregation (Grace Presbyterian Church, Franklin, NC)—some retired and one a high school student (who happened to be my son, Caleb, who was the first to suggest that I teach such a course in the first place!). Each member of the class had to purchase a New Testament Greek-English Interlinear before the class so that they could follow my Bible references in the Greek. After the class, I had each participant fill out an evaluation form. All agreed that the Greek prepositions were wonderful Gospel word pictures that they truly enjoyed learning. As one college student said about learning the Greek prepositions, "these allow me to go deeper in **t**ime **a**lone **w**ith **G**od (TAWG)." Another college student said the prepositions really "revealed the beauty and intricacy of the Greek New Testament." Also one retired women noted in the class that there was an "excitement of discovering the *richness* of meaning in the Greek New Testament." These blessed saints got it right—Greek can really help you in your own Time Alone With God to see the *richness* of God's word. This book *Impact Greek* is an outcome of that Bible study class held in the Great Smoky Mountains of North Carolina. So without further adieu; here's your introduction. Enjoy the intellectual discoveries and the spiritual impact of New Testament Greek.

Why did God choose Greek to communicate the Gospel of His Son?

The New Testament account of the life and power of our Lord Jesus Christ is all recorded in the Greek language. So why did God choose the Greek language to communicate the Gospel of His beloved Son? God worked providentially to prepare the Greek language in such a way that it could adequately communicate the story and glory of Jesus Christ, the Son of God. Consider this point from God the Father's perspective.[18] If you were imparting the truth about Jesus, wouldn't you choose a language which could communicate these precious accounts in an exceptional fashion? Wouldn't you desire the very best earthly language to communicate about your loved one? God certainly chose the very best language to proclaim to the world the truth of His Son. I believe God selected Greek due to its ability to communicate truth in a superior manner. As Kenneth S. Wuest has stated, "Greek is the most excellently equipped of the various languages spoken by men, and that is one of the reasons why God chose it for the New Testament language." In fact, I believe God chose Greek to communicate the Gospel for the following reasons:

1. Greek is an **emphatic** language.
2. Greek is an **educated** language.
3. Greek is an **evangelical** language.
4. Greek is an **exquisite** language.

These reasons are certainly not exhaustive, but they do give the reader an appreciation for why Greek is so useful to communicate heavenly truths. As Dr. Robertson, the great Greek grammarian, says, "The most perfect vehicle of human speech thus far devised by man is the Greek. English comes next, but Greek outranks it. The chief treasure in the

Greek language is the New Testament . . . The cultural and spiritual worth of the Greek New Testament is beyond all computation."[19]

Greek is an Emphatic Language

When Greek is described as an emphatic language it means that it communicates in a crisp, vivid and clear manner. It stands to reason that, if God were going to send His Son to die on the cross for our sins, He would want to make sure that all people understood Christ's cross in a clear, unambiguous manner. Greek was a perfect choice because it has this capacity.[20] In fact, at crucial teaching moments of the New Testament (such as the doctrine of the Deity of Christ), the Greek text reads with lawyer-like precision. Such a Divine Revelation demanded a precision and profoundness of thought that the Greek language provided. The famous Greek scholar, A.T. Robertson says, "The N.T. used the language of the people, but with a dignity, restraint and pathos far beyond . . . what is found in the remains of the ancient world" or in the records of our modern world.[21]

Greek is an Educated Language

Greek is a very ancient language that has a classical period as well as a common period. This makes it a very knowledgeable language that has considerable maturity. The classical period is represented by the works of Homer and the common period is reflected in the conquests of Alexander the Great. This long history gives the person writing Greek a versatility in communicating ideas that is second to none. On one hand, the classic period affords the Greek writer the substance to make fine and informative distinctions. On the other hand, the melting-pot-Greek of the common man gives the language a blunt, forthright style. For instance, it has been estimated that 80 percent of the Greek words used in the New Testament date from 322 B.C. God would certainly want to communicate His Son's vicarious atonement on the cross in a balanced manner, sophisticated but forthright. The Greek language was the best choice for this purpose.

Greek is an Evangelical Language

Certainly a God who so loved the world that He gave His only begotten son would choose a language that would facilitate the spread of this good news. Of course, Greek is such a language. It was the universal, international language of New Testament times. Most people at least knew some Greek as their second language. This fact made Greek a great vehicle for conveying the Gospel of God's Son. Furthermore, the influence of the Greek language on ancient cultures is revealed in certain historical phenomena. For example, the Romans (who spoke Latin) conquered the nation of Greece. Yet the Romans were persuaded to adopt the Greek language. A Latin poet wrote "captive Greece has taken captive her conqueror." Consequently, when Paul wrote to the church at Rome, he wrote in Greek not Latin. This is a piece of evidence that shows how thoroughly the Greek language had permeated the Roman culture. As a further example, consider the Jewish people. They loved their Hebrew Bible, the Old Testament, but that didn't stop a large section of Jews from translating the Hebrew O.T. into Greek. We know this version as the Septuagint or the LXX. In fact, the Septuagint was used by Jesus. Furthermore, the New Testament writers took 80 percent of their Old Testament quotes from the Greek LXX and not the Hebrew text[22] Dr. J. Julius Scott, Jr. notes "it is startling to learn that 40 percent of the pre-A.D. 70 burial inscriptions in Jerusalem are in Greek."[23] It is incredible that Greek has this power to persuade foreign people of its usefulness for their own endeavors—even to be placed on their tombstone. It is a language that draws converts to it. Dr. Robertson calls this facet "the eternal charm of the Greek language." What an excellent choice for God to use to spread the Good News of His Son, our Lord and Savior Jesus Christ.

Greek is an Exquisite Language

God would definitely want the inspired texts that tell us about His Son to become classics, written with an artistic flair. Greek is a language that has the capacity to express truths with creative finesse while still maintaining explicitness of meaning. Of course, Greek is tailor made for writing the great epics of history.

In giving us the New Testament, the Holy Spirit utilized the Greek language to show His eloquent skill as the Perfect Wordsmith. Consider the number of truly classic passages contained therein, all written in the Greek language by godly men who were moved along by the Holy Spirit (2 Peter 1:16). How could the moral foundation of the world survive without the four Gospels, the Sermon on the Mount or the Bible's love chapter (Paul's 1 Corinthians 13)? For instance, the Gospel of Luke has been described as the most beautiful writing in the world. Perhaps you don't believe this. Then consider the fact that only the Gospel of Luke has given such winsome parables as the Prodigal Son and the Good Samaritan. These are lovely masterpieces that rise to an unrivalled oratorical power and flow.

Purpose of this Book

The treasures of the Greek New Testament will sometimes take your breath away but at all times they will breathe fresh spiritual power into your soul. There is a joy found in the Greek New Testament that will impact your spiritual life in an amazing but real way. Here, then, is the purpose of this workbook: to edify God's people with a first hand look at some basic elements of the Greek of the New Testament. As His people come to this level of understanding, I believe they will also come to a deeper knowledge of Jesus, the Author and Finisher of their Faith.

This book is entitled, *"Impact Greek: The Joy and Power of the Greek New Testament."* My intent is to focus your mind and attention upon the power of the original Greek language of the New Testament so that you can experience its joy.

There are many introductory texts that discuss the Greek of the New Testament. Most of these books emphasize the academic side of learning the Greek language, which is indeed essential and helpful. However, many pastors throughout the years have taken Greek in seminary only to discontinue using it when they enter the ministry. Why? Perhaps they did not catch the communicative power of the Greek New Testament. Furthermore, why don't we teach the Greek language of the New Testament to those who sit in the pews each Sunday? Perhaps, it is considered too academically time consuming for these saints to learn a new language when they have to work full-time or raise a family (but, interestingly, the Jews still teach their children Hebrew). Unfortunately therefore, the impacting nature of the Greek text of the New Testament is missing from the life of most Christians. Can this lack of education be remedied? The famed Presbyterian preacher Dr. J. Gresham Machen (1881-1937) writes to fellow ministers:

> If, however, it (learning and reading Greek) is important for the minister (or the Christian bible student in the local church), what is to be done about it? Here we may come forward boldly with a message of hope. The Greek of the New Testament is by no means a difficult language; a very fair knowledge of it may be acquired by any minister (or Christian) of average intelligence.[24] (Words in parentheses added)

Dr. Machen then suggests that the minister read the Greek New Testament out loud each day as part of his daily devotion. He says, ". . . the Greek New Testament should be *read devotionally*. The Greek New Testament is a sacred book; and should be treated as such. If it is treated so, the reading of it will soon become a source of *joy* and power."[25] (Italics added) Did you catch that? If the Greek New Testament is read devotionally it will be a *source of joy*! This is exactly what this introduction is all about. To help the reader of the New Testament catch the joy of hearing the Holy Spirit's words as it is now faithfully recorded in the Greek of the New Testament. Dr. Robertson gives a welcome promise to us all when he says, "the Greek New Testament has a message for each mind." Aren't you intrigued to find out what that particular message is for *your* mind? No one in all of history expresses the true delight of knowing the Greek New Testament better than Erasmus who published a Greek N.T. almost five hundred years ago (A.D. 1516). He sums up his spiritual joy of reading the Greek New Testament in these words:

> These holy pages will summon up the living image of His mind. They will give Christ Himself, talking, healing, dying, rising, the whole Christ in a word; they will give Him to you in an intimacy so close that He would be less visible to you if he stood before your eyes.

To help you understand and experience the impact of the Greek New Testament we will proceed as follows:

- You will learn how the Greeks were experts at saying "No"—that is NO!—in their language. This is a thrilling look inside the Greek New Testament, which will show you the impacting power of this wise language.

- You will learn the H.O.P.E. Bible Study System and the O.P.E.N. Journal method, which will provide you an organized way to glean treasures from the Greek New Testament.

This study is about the joy of the Holy Spirit in the believer's heart. This joy is often conveyed through His creative word choice and use in the majestic, marvelous record of the New Testament. *Impact Greek* is referring to the power of the Holy Spirit to use the Greek of the New Testament to penetrate the Christian's heart in order to move it to joy—eternal joy! The famous question from The Westminster Shorter Catechism asks, "What is the chief end of man?" The answer is, "Man's chief end is to glorify God, and to enjoy him forever." The Greek New Testament helps us fulfill our highest calling to glorify and enjoy God forever. Martin Luther, John Calvin and John Wesley of Reformation fame all knew this truth and practiced reading the Greek New Testament. Even John Knox, at the age of fifty, was motivated to learn to read the Greek behind the biblical text. Pope Leo X encouraged Erasmus to publish the Greek New Testament. He did and the world changed for the better. Robertson observes that:

> The Greek New Testament, scattered over Europe by the printing press, had produced a spiritual earthquake. The darkness began to vanish from the world when the Greek New Testament was allowed to shed its light . . . The Greek New Testament is still the Torchbearer of Light and Progress for the world.

The impact of Greek is undeniable. It started the Reformation. It also can reform *you*.[26]